The Best Book on How to Start Over: Rebuild Your Mind, Body & Finances

by Zackary Richards

Ari Publishing

Hello and welcome. You're likely reading this because Life hit you with a truck, backed up, ran over you again then rifled through your pockets, took all your money and left you broken and bleeding in the road. That happened to me too.

First piece of advice. Stop trying to figure out *why* it happened. It doesn't matter. What does matter is you've got to drag your broken and bleeding body out of the street before another truck comes along.

It is a fact that nature HATES weakness so unless you want the life's predators to start zeroing in on you, you need to get out of the line of fire.

Since I have no idea what circumstances brought you here, I cannot fine tune the instructions to directly apply to your situation. What I can do however, is provide a roadmap to show you how _you_ can turn things around.

So question #1: Is you present circumstances worth salvaging? Your situation is serious or you wouldn't be reading this so, instead of running around trying to fix everything and making yourself crazy, step back for a moment and ask yourself if what you presently have or about to lose is really worth keeping.

And this is no easy question. If money is the problem, but you have a loving family & friends then keep plugging away. Money problems eventually end. You either recover or file for bankruptcy and start over. It's rough and humiliating but you aren't the first to hit the financial wall (Donald Trump filed for bankruptcy twice) and won't be the last to build their finances back up again.

If it's health problems, that also usually (but not always) gets resolved one way or the other. You undergo whatever treatment is necessary, (because you don't have a choice) then, just like rebuilding your finances, you rebuild your body until it's completely healthy again. It is often a terrifying and painful experience, however once you recover, there is a very good chance you'll be as good as new.

If it's an emotional problems, say your spouse betrayed you, or your child is on drugs, or you have no friends and feel worthless, that too can be overcome. Again, it will be a painful experience but eventually, you will win out.

But what if it's far worse than any of those examples? What if everything is or has gone wrong and at a pace you can't possibly keep up with? What if you're being battered from all sides with no end in sight?

Yeah, now we're talking.

And maybe some of it (or maybe all of what's happened) is your fault. Maybe none of it is. Again, it doesn't matter. The first mistake I made when my former life blew up was to constantly review what had happened, piece by piece, inch by inch, all in horrific detail to try and find out what went wrong. Maybe it could be fixed.

I still had hope.

That was mistake # 2. Why? Because that was my ego talking. I believed I was clever enough to fix everything. I was sure I could turn it all around. I was miserable, bitter, lonely and damn near suicidal yet I kept believing it would all turn out all right if I just kept at it.

And if you keep believing that, Life will simply keep beating you until you finally wake up and realize this is one war you're not going to win.

So here are your choices. Keep fighting until you are broken, beaten and humiliated or accept the fact that once you've given it your best, done all you can and nothing has improved, it's time for a change.

And this realization can be frightening, you will be unsure, you will question your every decision. What if it all goes wrong?

Can it be any worse than it is now?

Just how much misery do you think you can take before you snap and have to be dragged off to some mental healthcare facility?

So it's decision time. Stay out there in the street dodging the heavy traffic life throws at you or say nuts to this, step up on the sidewalk and begin planning your new life.

That's right. Part two of your life is waiting for the new you to show up. So stop torturing yourself up with old platitudes like *'Winners never quit & quitters never win'*, and all that rah, rah, rah, go team go, BS.

Comedian W.C Fields once addressed this attitude by saying *'If at first you don't succeed, try, try again...and then give up. No sense being a damn fool about it.'*

Many self-help tutorials focus on the spiritual and ask you to turn your life over to GOD. This method has been highly successful for alcoholics and drug addicts so by all means consider it.

BUT as the old saying goes *God helps those who help themselves* so since you've already started down that path I'm going to provide you with some additional instruction so God won't have to work as hard.

This book is broken into three parts, The Mind, the Body and the Finances. Because people whose lives have crashed and burned, often had their emotional, physical and financial health crash and burn as well.

In the first section THE MIND you will learn to change your way of thinking and your way of addressing problems. You will see that by adopting new methods brings new successes. You will learn what works and why and what methods need to be changed.

None of it is difficult to learn but it will require action on your part, and a lot of it. And when you do take action you will discover that the happiness you experience when you dream about success is nothing compared to the happiness you will experience when you actually become a success.

You will also learn that becoming a success isn't evil or bad. You won't turn into some moneygrubbing miser. In fact, you will become a far more effective person because you will have the wherewithal to actually DO SOMETHING for those in need instead of just squeezing a dollar bill into the Salvation Army's Christmas pot during the holiday season.

In the second section, The Body you will learn to change what you eat and the reason you need to do so. And no, it won't consist of some Spartan diet or insane exercise plan that will make you miserable. What you will learn is what foods best nourish your body, speed up your metabolism and strengthen your immune system so you can add them to your daily diet. You will also learn how to successfully quit smoking and what exercises bring about the best results in the shortest amount of time.

In the third section Finances, you will learn what has really happened to the economy, how it affects you and what steps you'll need to take to create additional income so money concerns will no longer be a major problem.

First, I'm going to debunk some more old myths and sanctimonious platitudes. In particular that old saw that states, *You make your own luck.*

No you don't.

You are either lucky or you aren't lucky.

Some people are extremely lucky. They just are. You likely know someone like that. They always happen to be at the right place at the right time. They were born attractive, to good parents, received a good education, and met the right people who helped them on their way. Things always seem to work out for them.

I am not one of those people. I suspect you aren't either.

And I'm not knocking them. They no doubt worked very hard to achieve what they got. They put in the hours, made the sacrifices and did all that was necessary to come out on top.

So what have they got that we ain't got? The opportunity!

Napoleon once said "Ability is nothing without opportunity."

Like you, I worked my tail off. Put in long hours, made sacrifices, did all I was supposed to do.

And it all fell apart anyway.

So much for making your own luck. And it REALLY annoys me off when I'm watching one of the late night talk shows and some actor tells this story of how they were discovered. "I was sitting at home when an actor friend called and asked if I would like to go with them to an audition, and on the way help them go over their lines. I had nothing else planned so I said sure. We arrive, she auditions and afterward is asked to fill out some paperwork in another office. So as I'm waiting for her to return, some guys sticks his head out of the door, points to me and says, 'C'mon, you're next!' As I go over and am about to explain that I'm not an actor, he hands me a script and asks me to read to some guy sitting in a chair. Then I saw it was same lines I had read to my friend. So I shrugged, read the lines and was asked to do it again. So I did and was then told I had gotten the part. So I was cast and the show ran for seven seasons!

I won't reveal the actors name but that's a true story.

So the woman with absolutely no experience, and no training, got the job her friend, the experienced, properly trained professional actor had auditioned for just by agreeing to go along for a ride. Again, so much for making your own luck.

I once worked for a very successful man, a top notch businessman and he said the formula for success is to find out what it is you want to do, become the best there is at that particular discipline and work non-stop until you achieve your goal.

OR," he added. "Just be lucky and the rest won't matter."

Words to live by.

However, it's probably safe to say that like me, you aren't particularly lucky.

That doesn't mean you can't become fortunate. It doesn't mean you've been knocked out of the game of life and have nothing to look forward to other than a lonely tragic death. Seriously. Lighten up, it's going to get better. Trust me.

Tom Petty once sang "Even the losers get lucky sometimes" Now I'm not saying we're losers, I'm saying we're not all that lucky. And the good news is I've discovered ways to cash in on the few opportunities when they do arrive.

How?

I started by trying to figure out how to win at a competition where luck factors in more than most anything else, but doesn't have too many unknowns or variables to influence the outcome. What competition fits that bill? Poker. Now don't think I'm going to suggest you make money gambling. Not at all. This example is for observational purposes only. So you can see that there are real opportunities in instances when math overrides luck.

I'm a good Texas Hold 'em Poker Player. And you would never know it if you saw the cards I'm regularly dealt. I fold early and often. BUT, sooner or later the law of averages catches up and I find myself looking at a good hand. Do I go all in?

Nope. I've folded with two aces before the flop on many occasions, usually because someone has raised with a considerable amount of money or has gone 'All in". Since I know there are a number of combinations that can beat a pair of aces, and with 5 new cards to be drawn there are 5 chances someone else at the table will draw a better hand and since I know I'm not all that lucky, I'll wait until the odds are more in my favor. And MOST importantly, I don't permit my ego, sense of competition or delusions of instant riches factor into my betting decisions. I ONLY move when the odds of me having the best hand is very high.

And even then I bet cautiously, see if any of my opponents get overenthusiastic and careless because I don't. Once I'm sure I will likely win I slowly match them and raise just a little to make them think I am unsure and therefore keep raising.

In those cases where I wind up ahead, it usually isn't by that much because of all the money I lost by folding in previous hands, but it's almost always more than I when I started.

Gambling, is very much like life. How often you win depends on how well you play the game.

By playing cautiously and observing my opponents, I know who bluffs and who doesn't, who is reckless and who is lucky. And as the saying goes. Knowledge is power. Since I've never been able to depend on luck, I've developed my skills and so I don't need luck... I got math instead.

Since I only became involved to test my theory, the amount won didn't matter. What mattered was that my theory worked. Math can override luck if you do it correctly.

I don't gamble anymore. It's too time consuming and I can make a lot more money doing other things where luck isn't such a large factor. Plus there is always the possibility the gambling bug may bite and if you're looking to utterly destroy your life, that's an almost guaranteed way to do it.

But businesswise, making small regular profits may not seem like much but they add up. Big wins are rare and hard to come by even for lucky people but small regular wins are common and once you've discovered what does work, it becomes easier to do it again and again. Small wins aren't flashy and because they don't attract a lot of interest, most people pass. Create enough of them however and you'll have a steady additional income stream month after month.

And you won't need luck to do it.

But that's the happy ending. Before I got to that point I had to make many changes in my attitude, in my appearance and how I thought of myself. What I am going to show you is that there are ways to win without luck. No, you will probably not be as fortunate as those whom life favors, but the next time Life's truck comes gunning for you, you'll see it coming and be well out of its way when it roars by.

So let's get started on those changes.

First choose a day, say next Monday for example. And on that day you are going to put your past and everything terrible that comes with it in the trash. On that day you're not going to think about it anymore, you're not going to worry about it anymore and you're not going to let it into your life anymore.

***Note* I am NOT suggesting you quit your job or abandon your family. The goal here is to start**

addressing the problems that are ruining your life and do whatever is necessary to put an end to them. But do it both legally and morally.

Do everything you have to do to make this happen. Don't drag it out. Confer with whatever business or legal professionals necessary to protect your interests then get it done. Over with. Finished!

THE END

Chapter 1 of your new life: Here's how you begin: When you get up on that Monday, you start the day by viewing a positive reinforcement video from people like Tony Robbins, Zig Ziglar, Napoleon Hill, Les Brown, Wayne Dyer etc. on www.YouTube.com And REMEMBER the core of what they are all saying. **You become what you tell yourself you are**. When things go wrong, DO NOT say things to yourself like, "I'm such a loser. Why does everything I touch turn to crap? I can't seem to do anything right. Why does everything always go wrong for me?"

Studies have shown that the brain programs itself with the information it receives. If you consistently tell yourself you're a loser, you will subconsciously act in that manner.

If you instead give yourself positive reinforcement, and adopt a "you'll get 'em next time champ," mentality you will begin to believe you will and the more you do it, the more your life will improve. Start each day by telling yourself that you're going to turn things around and life will be better than ever before.

Super successful internet marketer Vick Strizheus absolutely refuses ANY negativity to be around him. He tells his students from the very beginning that if they've come with the attitude that they probably won't succeed, he'll immediately refund their money and show them the door.

Once you start following the instructions from these self-help gurus you'll notice that they all preach the same thing, in order to be successful you first must convince yourself that *you can do* it, *believe that you can do it* and then *go ahead and just do it.*

You will also notice that many of the success stories told on those videos start with that person at the end of their rope. Vick starts his story by explaining that when he started he was $30,000 in debt, had a family and no income. Others worked several low-paying jobs and still couldn't support their families. There were those devastated by divorce or the death of a loved one. Still more were shattered by natural disasters. Some suffered serious illness and others were literally homeless.

The point is many others have been where you are now and they hunkered down, started over and created a life that made them happy and fulfilled. I did it by following the same information I will be giving you in this book.

But none of it will work until you decide and believe you *can* succeed, that you *will* overcome and create the life you've worked so hard for. So that's where we stand, friend. I can show you how to start over and build a new and better life. What you need to do is decide you're going to do it.

You are not going to give it your best shot. You are not going to give it a whirl. You are not going to try your best because that's a loser mentality. If you think you might fail then you are already preparing yourself to do so. Like Yoda once said, "You either do or do not. There is no try." And this time you will succeed because you will know what to do when things go wrong.

And you WILL NOT STOP UNDER ANY CIRCUMSTANCES. YOU WILL EITHER SUCCEED OR KEEL OVER DEAD AT YOUR DESK.

Your future is completely up to you. There is no one else responsible for your success, no one to blame, no one to look to for help, no one to give you a break. It's just you, your brains, your muscle and most of all, your determination.

Your old unhappy life is over. Do whatever is necessary to extricate yourself from it. Get rid of anything that reminds you of it. And if that means distancing yourself from old friends, then do so. If that means taking a new job, then do it, if that means moving to another city, then start packing. Box the old photos and store them away.

I'm not going to regale you with my personal tale of woe, because frankly I don't see why you would care and if we're going to do this then there needs to be less talk and more action.

So am I to assume you've made up your mind to start a new life?

If so, that great! But remember it will not be easy. Nothing worth accomplishing ever is. But then again, that makes victory all the sweeter!

So let's start with Phase 1

Phase One: Rebuilding Your Way of Thinking.

If you are going to be successful you will need to think like successful people. There is no need to reinvent the wheel. Nothing I teach in this book is outrageously innovative. However, these techniques have worked for countless people and it will likely work for you.

But here's the catch. There are many methods of self-improvement and you have to find the one that talks to you. The method makes you say, *Oh, that makes sense! So that's why that works! Yes, I can do that!* And it isn't easily found. So each morning when you watch the positive reinforcement tutorials on YouTube, view a different speaker. You can start with Tony Robbins, then Zig Ziglar then Napoleon Hill and so on, then rinse and repeat until you find the method and teacher you want to use. But don't overdo it.

Just one a day. Each and EVERY DAY!

Write down methods that make sense to you. By writing them down your brain will better remember them and start reprogramming them into your daily actions.

Here's another important piece of information. You MUST learn to block negative thoughts.

21

Because you have been beating yourself up for so long, this will not be easy, but you *can* do it. Like a drunk whose first reaction is to reach for a drink when things get bad, negative thinkers often fall back on negative thinking when things go wrong until they are reprogrammed into positive thinkers. That is why it's so important to do it every day because, just as vices become habits after a few weeks, positive reinforcements become positive actions.

Look at this process as if you were starting a new job. You go for training, study what you've learned and then by doing, become good at the job. This works the same way. In fact this method is superior because it teaches you how to be a better you.

Overtime you will notice that you are becoming more confident, more relaxed in your own skin, better able to handle stress and difficult situations. You become more focused, and learn to laser target your goals.

The majority of people are having a very difficult time trying to figure life out. We are constantly barraged by TV, movies and other forms of entertainment that are designed to make us feel good and that assure us that everything will work out in the end. So we wander around like happy idiots, brainwashed into believing that the underdog will win in the end, the guy who tries the hardest and is honest and true will be rewarded and the prettiest girl will fall for the pimple-faced nerd because he's nice to her when her jock boyfriend hurts her feelings.

Does it ever happen? Possibly. Maybe once in a blue moon. But you want to know what happens most of the time? The underdog loses horribly, the guy who tries hardest and is honest and true gets fired due to office politics and the prettiest girl kisses the nerd on the cheek, tells him he's such a great guy then runs back into the arms of her abusive jock boyfriend.

But…but… That's not fair!

No, it isn't but in order to succeed you must first understand what you are dealing with. People will follow those who are confident and self-assured; those who have become successful and live that lifestyle. That is the person you need to become. Not the soft-hearted, always there for you, best buddy.

When my daughter was in college she told me she wanted to become a social worker because she wanted to help the downtrodden. I sat her down and explained that a social worker makes little money, spends most of their time petitioning the government for funds and resources and are saddled with dealing with the drug addled and mentally ill. I said if she wanted to help the poor and downtrodden then take business courses and learn how to become rich, because people like Bill Gates and Warren Buffet can do more for the unfortunate with a single donation than a thousand social workers can do in a lifetime.

Now let's address what's wrong with you. Unlike Mr. Rogers, very few people will like you just the way you are. If you believe it's what's inside that counts, then you asking people to judge you by looking at what they cannot see.

Remember that adage *'You never get a second chance to make a first impression?'* Well you don't. So have a look at your wardrobe. Still wearing hoodies? Jeans? Sneakers?

People who wear hoodies, jeans and sneakers when not doing yard work are people of leisure. They don't need to dress because they don't need to meet and network with successful people. They've made their money and are enjoying the fruits of their labor.

Wait, you say *you* wear hoodies, jeans and sneakers and are not a person of leisure? Well stop doing that! Suit up, or pantsuit up, my friend. Because people who dress for success are treated like they are successful.

Case in point, if you go into a high end store dressed well, the sales personnel will treat you like a king or queen. You can ask all kinds of questions and they will happily answer because you look like someone who will buy something.

If however you go into that same store dressed in a washed out hoodie, worn jeans and sneakers, you will be treated dismissively and ignored.

If you are treated like crap you will begin to feel like crap and that's what we're trying to avoid. So start each day with a shower, shave, your daily positive reinforcement video and if not business attire, at the very least, a collared shirt and sports jacket. For the ladies a collared blouse, slacks and optional jacket.

Remember, you are somebody. Dress and act like it.

If money is tight there are consignment stores that sell used clothing in great condition. Check for clearance sales or Going out of Business sales. I once bought a sports jacket that originally sold for $125 dollars for $12 and a $450 dollar suit for $60. And if you don't know where to start, ask Google.

There are many places on the net that sell extremely discounted goods from odd lots and over purchases.

Next Step: Filter out inappropriate language.

I know, life can be very frustrating and the urge to drop the F-bomb can be very tempting. It certainly was for me because I was born in the Bronx where inappropriate language is pretty much the coin of the realm.

But remember, you are starting fresh. There is absolutely nothing to be gained by using inappropriate language. Plus there are those who are offended when you take God's name in vain or refer to someone as a flaming shithead. Acquire the things that benefit you, that make you look better than the unwashed masses, more accomplished than the guy or gal down the street.

And by this I don't mean "keeping up with the Jones's" I mean getting the accessories that present you as someone who is on the fast track to success.

For example: a friend of mine who was starting her own business, purchased a high mileage older BMW. The body however looked pristine, almost new although it was over a decade old. She later told me that showing up in a BMW got her more clients than her late model Volkswagen ever would have.

I have discovered that in order to be happy it is important to accept life as it really is. Take the time to note what is real and what isn't. We are spoon fed feel-good platitudes throughout life and unfortunately, fall victim into believing them. In the race between the turtle and the hare, the hare wins. Old age and treachery WILL defeat youth and enthusiasm, nice guys DO finish last and Gold does make the rules.

Your options are as follows. You can play life by its own rules or you can bemoan cruel fate. Life isn't fair. It cheats, it lies, it betrays. Accept that fact. Because life is a hell of a lot fairer to those who don't allow themselves to be deluded into thinking that it will all turn out all right just because you're a good person.

Remember: just because you don't eat lion, doesn't mean the lion won't eat you.

This is not to say that in order to become a success, you must become a grasping, despicable Scrooge like character. Not at all. Just stop telling yourself that you are taking the high road by refusing to get down and dirty with those who also want what you want. This is business. They are your competition.

They are the enemy. They will take whatever is yours right from under your nose if you let them.

So don't let them.

Next step: Refine your attitude

It's human nature to want to be liked. Yet people who clearly want to be liked are considered needy and to be avoided. Seems like a no-win situation. And in a way it is. So since there is no way to please everybody, focus on pleasing the people who can improve your situation. Successful people are no better or smarter than you. They simply learned to do a particular task relatively well. And just because a person is good at a particular profession doesn't automatically mean they'll know what to do when disaster strikes. You could be the best bus driver in America but how is that going to help when the engine dies and catches fire?

If we learned anything from the 2008-2009 financial meltdown it's that those so-called financial professionals were as lost and confused as the rest of us. So don't be intimidated by fame or fortune. Successful people want to meet other successful people and will welcome you into the fold if you have something to offer.

And when starting out all you may have to offer is being interesting and fun to have around. Fun and interesting people are especially welcome in successful circles because so many of them are hard core realists, whose main focus is money. There are services that literally 'rent out' people who are particularly interesting and entertaining to lighten the mood and engage the attendees at weddings, conferences and other social events when it's important that everyone has a good and memorable time.

Successful people avoid those looking for a hand out or a leg up yet have nothing to offer in return.

<u>Don't be that person.</u>

So are you interesting and engaging? No? Then why not? It isn't hard. All it takes is a little study and practice.

So here's what you need to know.

As a writer I know that the thing people want most is content. They want to know things that most other people don't know so they can appear knowledgeable and smugly superior. They also want to hear *clever* jokes they can use to entertain others, again to make themselves look witty and interesting.

Because, let's face it. Everybody loves the life of the party!

Okay, let's say you're not particularly interesting or funny. Here's how to fix that. Buy several notebooks (like the ones kids take to school) and mark them 'Interesting Facts, Funny Jokes, Engaging Stories, Great Quotes & Business Trends'

Then do your homework. Go on the internet or library and gather information to write into those books and again I say WRITE because the brain better remembers information when you write it down. Collect interesting facts, funny jokes, engaging stories etc. Fill those notebooks and refer to them regularly.

In fact, the internet has websites that do nothing but provide Interesting Facts, Funny Jokes, Engaging stories etc. And there is a distinct advantage in NOT being a naturally funny or engaging person because those type of people often get carried away and wind up looking more like a clown than a witty conversationalist.

To appear clever, simply add an interesting fact to each conversation, a joke here and there, and an engaging story and you're all set. You'll appear sharp and on the ball yet still professional enough to be taken seriously.

Once you've established yourself as an interesting person, solidify that impression by asking prominent people about themselves. Successful people _**love**_ to talk about how they became successful people. They also love to give advice. So ask them what they think a person like you should focus on to become more successful. (Don't say _financially_ successful, they will hear that as you requesting free financial advice)

And more times than not they will offer direction you can readily use.

They didn't become successful by being stupid, so be sure to listen.

So where do you find these people?

Seminars.

Back when I worked for corporate I was sent to training seminars at least twice a year. And I always found them interesting and informative. Here are some of the benefits

Live training on the topics you want to specialize in.

You get the latest and most up to date information.

Meet people and network.

Talk to accomplished professionals and pick their brains.

There is a site that lists seminars around the country

Go to www.nationalseminarstraining.com for details.

Should you attend, have business cards made. You'll want to have one available should you be asked. Many solid and profitable contacts are made at these functions so if you can, get to one whenever possible.

Also attending conferences and seminars makes you appear as a person who stays on top of things. As a person who takes his/her career seriously. Perhaps a beneficial contact to have somewhere down the line. Become that person.

Other places to network is the Free Masons, the Knights of Columbus, the Benevolent & Protective Order of Elks and other fraternal organizations.

Zig Ziglar says: **If you want to succeed at something, help others succeed at what they're doing.**

There is excellent math in that saying. If you simply focus on improving **your**self and **your** circumstances you become a one man band. One person alone and in battle. But if you pass along what you've learned to those also looking to succeed, once they've achieved their goals they will likely help you and the more people you help the more will help you.

You will then have an army of the experienced battling alongside you.

And there is another important factor involved here. When you help others it takes your mind off your problems and reinforces your core belief that you are a good person and deserving of a good and happy life.

In the movie the Shawshank Redemption, Morgan Freeman's character says "You got two choices, you can get busy living or get busy dying."

When you think about it, that *is* what life is all about. When my life blew up I finally realized that returning to an empty apartment each night shellshocked and in the middle of a financial and emotional super storm was only asking for more trouble. Cutting yourself off from people when your life is crumbling will only make things worse. Your life will become your problems.

And that's no life at all.

So taking Morgan Freeman's advice I decided to get busy living. I made up my mind not to go home after work and instead find something interesting to do. I scoured the Arts & Entertainment section of my city's newspaper and found local events and began attending them. Many were colossal bores but some were very interesting and engaging. I met new people (which wasn't easy as I am very introverted) made new friends and adopted new interests.

And during that time I wasn't obsessing over my problems but instead was having a surprisingly good time. You're in the middle of the fight of your life. Don't just stand there and take a beating. MOVE! Stick and jab. Don't sit there waiting for the executioner to arrive. Because the truth is The Executioner WILL arrive for us all sooner or later, so what good does it do to sit around and wait?

And another advantage is that you might meet someone who has already gone through the same thing you are going through and may be able to help. But remember, nobody wants to listen to a stranger's tale of woe. They have their own issues to deal with. So be personable and friendly and if asked what's going on in your life, respond by giving a one sentence synopsis. For example: *I'm in the middle of digging myself out of some bad financial decisions* or *My marriage is on the rocks* or *My kid is having trouble with the law.* If there is one thing I have learned (and I'm sure you have too) is that Life is full of surprises. And you never know. The person you're talking with might just so happen to be a financial expert or marriage counselor or attorney

Don't waste time and energy.

Prioritize. Each day (after viewing your positive reinforcement video) decide what actions will bring the most results that day and do them first. Too often we like to begin our work day by doing the tasks that we don't mind doing and then easing into the harder stuff. When you do that however, you are pushing the most effective and progress making actions to the back of the line and by the time we get to them we are already tired and unenthusiastic.

As Dr. Phil often says: *How's that working out for you?*

The purpose of restarting your life is to become the person you want to be and do the work you want to do. Regardless of what field you chose there WILL be parts of it that are boring or distasteful. That is unavoidable so it's best to tackle those tasks first. By doing the things that bring the most results

__FIRST__ you automatically lower the time it will take for you to see marked improvement. **There is nothing more valuable than your time.**

As you consider what you want to do with the rest of your life always factor in the realities of life and of business. Don't pick a field that is already saturated. There are highly experienced people already established there and as a new comer you certainly aren't ready to go head-to-head with them.

One of the surest paths to success is to find a profitable niche and find something in it that niche that hasn't already been exploited.

A perfect example is what Stephen Jobs did with Apple. He didn't just go head to head with Bill Gates' Microsoft. He found other uses for the technology and made billions doing so. iTunes & iPods for example. Many don't know this but he was heavily invested in Pixar which revolutionized the animated movie industry.

These super successful people often became rich by simply asking themselves what would I really like to have that doesn't exist yet? And it doesn't have to be something complex. Look at those product on *As Seen on TV*. Many of those products fill a very simple, yet common need. That magnetic mesh screen to keep the bugs out for example. The Snuggie for another and many others. These simple yet popular products only reinforce my claim that you don't have to be exceptionally clever or educated to become a success. The only thing you really need is desire, tenacity and perseverance.

Do not suffer fools gladly

Successful people are immediate turned off by complainers. They feel that if something didn't work out for you then you did something wrong. Lucky people don't believe in luck because they've never experienced truly bad luck. They worked hard and eventually, because they were lucky, positive things started happening.

We all judge life by our personal experiences and since that was their experience as well as the experience of their also lucky friends, they believe that if you worked as hard as they did, you would get the same results. Because these people *are* lucky and things almost always work out for them, they don't understand that there are people for whom things rarely work out for.

I can tell you from personal experience that there are exceedingly brilliant and talented people among us who you will never hear of and whose incredible abilities will either never be known or not be discovered until they're dead. People who have worked just as hard and, in many instances, much harder than the lucky ones, yet they never made it to the right place at the right time.

Don't believe me? How about Vincent Van Gogh? Gregor Mendel, El Greco, Steig Larson? Just to name a few.

Such is life. But then again, they didn't know how to successfully market their talents and, friend, if you are truly determined to become a success, remember this above all things, **MARKETING IS THE MOST IMPORTANT KEY TO YOUR SUCCESS!**

One of the biggest mistakes a person can make is to assume that because you have a terrific product, service or knowledge, that fact, in and of itself, will insure success.

No it won't.

You may have designed and created the most effective and powerful cannon in existence but if you aim it in the wrong direction it will fail. And that's what marketing is. Aiming your product (or yourself for that matter) at the people who want to see it, want to learn about it and most of all, want to buy it.

So let's take a moment to review what we've covered so far. You've decided to start a new life. You've begun watching an inspirational video every morning, are dressing like a successful person and have learned that you don't need luck to be successful, you just need to learn to do the things that will **make** you successful and how to meet the people who can show you how it's done. It is likely you will read this book several times, which is a good idea to see just how much you've accomplished and if you missed anything. But the most important part of review is to evaluate how much of you and your life has permanently changed. Because if the answer is 'not much' then you can expect the same horrors you experienced before to visit you again. Ergo the old saying *'The definition of insanity is to do the same thing over and over and expect different results.'*

Who you were and who you are becoming are two distinctly different people. Your old friends won't likely fit into your new life, nor will they fit in with your new friends. Why? Because misery loves company and well, if you've carried out all the directions in this book you're no longer miserable. In fact, you're likely quite happy. And there are many reasons for this. Successful people don't worry all the time. They're not concerned about paying the mortgage, or making their next car payment. They can afford to take their spouse or their significant other to an expensive restaurant and not care how much it will cost. Their car is in top shape and their house is in a good neighborhood and their kids go to good schools.

And no, their lives aren't trouble free. No matter how lucky you are, Life knocks everybody around now and then. The only difference is that with successful people there isn't as much opportunity to do so because they have most of their bases covered. They have excellent healthcare, see their doctors and dentists regularly, they eat properly and exercise, pay their bills on time and are fully insured to prevent lawsuits or to replace stolen or damaged property. They have friends with influence and pull and when stressed can simply book a flight to any tropical paradise they chose.

Sure beats the hell out of sweating rent and praying your vehicle holds out until you've paid it off. Or wondering if that lump you've discovered is something serious. Or being afraid to take your family on vacation because of all the lay-offs.

Evaluate your friends

Write down the names of your friends. Then ask yourself, if you were invited to meet the President of the United States and could bring a friend, which ones would you offer that opportunity? The ones you wouldn't are the ones you need to cut. We all have that goofball friend who is fun but never grew up. Financially, he or she is holding on by their fingernails and is one or two paychecks away from being homeless. He or she is in their thirties yet acts like they're still in their teens. They got the stink of failure all over them and sooner or later when it all goes down they're going to drag you with them.

Don't let that happen.

Yeah we still love Johnnie Jackass, Freaky Freddy and Slutty Sally but you're not doing yourself or them any favors by sticking around until it all comes apart. You can much better serve yourself *and them* by focusing on turning your fortunes around first and then once you've got the life you wanted, see if you can help them get theirs.

Remember the advice I gave my daughter when she wanted to help the downtrodden? Well the same goes here. You'd be a much better friend if you were in a position to help them turn their life around rather than hanging out with them until Life's truck turns them into road kill.

41

Evaluate your Family

Do the same with them that you did with your friends. If they don't pass the test then it's time to put those relationships on the back burner. Too often we become the one everyone else relies on when there is yet another family crisis or emergency. Ask yourself this question, what type of help or assistance would they provide if you were in serious trouble?

If the answer is little to none, they are just using you.

Stop letting them do that.

In fact, you might consider adopting a new nickname when you roll out this new you. If your name is William and were nicknamed Bill or Billy, consider reintroducing yourself to your new people as Will. Or if your name is Alexander and were nicknamed Al you might want to consider Alex or Lex. Or if your name is Tiffany and were nicknamed Tiff consider switching to Anny. The new you has a new attitude, a new wardrobe and a new personality so you might like a new name to go with it.

Paul Simon once sang *"When I look back on all the crap I learned in high school it's a wonder I can think at all."*

We're taught from childhood to get a good education so that we can find a good job.

Translation: Become valuable to someone else so they can work you to death to make their own financial dreams come true. Because that's what we had to do and why should your life be any better?

All it really boils down to is this: Do you want to work to make your own dreams come true. OR do you want to work to make someone else's dreams come true?

Let me first state that there is absolutely nothing wrong with working for someone else. The question is, are you adequately paid for your services? Do you like the work you do? Are you the type who prefers a steady paycheck and benefits to risking it all to seek your fortune?

When I worked for corporate things were very simple. I showed up for work on time every day, did my assigned tasks, worked well with my associates and did my best to help the company prosper.

In return I was well paid, treated with respect, received full health benefits, a matching 401K, had life insurance, worked a 40 hour week, had weekends off, paid holidays, a steady paycheck and a pleasant working environment. Come 5 o'clock I went home leaving the work concerns at the office.

Today I am self-employed and work 70 hours a week, 7 days a week, no 401K, no steady paycheck, (although some weeks are MUCH better than others) and no life insurance and I spend most of my waking hours thinking about my business.

But I am much happier.

Why? Because no one gets to decide when I wake up in the morning, what to wear when I go out, what time to eat my lunch, how far to drive each day, what tasks I must perform and so on.

I work 70 hours because I WANT TO. I love what I do. I start work around 10 o'clock each morning, take a break somewhere in the afternoon, work some more, eat dinner then go back to work until some television show comes on that I want to see. I rarely know (or care) what day it is because it doesn't matter. I have no Blue Mondays, Hump days or TGIF's. One evening I was so involved in writing this book when I finally checked the time I discovered it was 3 am.

And what I really like is that each month I do a little better financially.

But you see, that's just me. I'm naturally a night person. Back in corporate I had to wake up at 6 am, five days a week, drive over 50 miles there and back and often during snowstorms and blizzards. But I had a family to support.

So I did it.

As the saying goes. If I only knew then what I knew now.

You on the other hand might be a day person and be up and ready to start the day at the crack of dawn. Have a 5-10 minute commute. Love your work and the people you work with and for.

You are living the dream, buddy. So ride that little red wagon until the wheels fall off.

A word to the wise however, the end of the line may be closer than you think. But more on that later.

Unfortunately, we are all led to believe that business owners are somehow better and superior to everyone else. They must be because everyone treats them with respect and defers to their judgment.

Why? Because you never know when you might need to ask them for a job.

Think back on your childhood. How often were you encouraged to start your own business? Encouraged to follow your dreams, or follow your own path? Probably not much.

This is why you need to start your new life. The information you grew up with may have been good advice in the past but it's not good advice now.

Take a real good and hard look at the reality we're presenting living in. Human beings as physical workers are quickly becoming obsolete.

Within 15 years the business models we use today will likely be gone, and their employees with them.

But more on that when we get to the finance section.

Learn to deal with rejection.

Of all the lessons I had to learn, dealing with rejection was the hardest. That's primarily because I'm an egomaniac and take any form of rejection as a personal attack and a hate crime.

So I had to change that. If you come to someone with an offer or business plan or product and they aren't interested, they aren't rejecting you, they are rejecting the business offer. If you opened a pizzeria and someone walked by, looked at your pizza in the window and you smiled and they smiled back and walked away, they don't hate you. They just don't want pizza right now.

Another advantage of risking rejection is that, although the person you make the offer to may not be interested, they may know someone who might be. **OR** have a suggestion on how to improve your offer or an idea on how to better market it.

Comedian Joan Rivers, who has been a staple on TV since the 1960s credits her continuing popularity to this belief. "If you want lightning to strike, you need to be out there in the storm." And she's right. If you want to be successful, then people need to know who you are and so you need to introduce yourself to them.

I understand that many people are naturally shy, some even cripplingly so. But shyness can be overcome and there are several self-help books and audio books that address that topic and provide the techniques you'll need to overcome it.

Remember you are rebuilding yourself from the ground up.

One of the personality flaws I carried around for the better part of my life was my tendency to speak my mind without considering the effect my words might have on someone.

I wasn't intentionally cruel. I just felt it was easier and more effective to cut to the point and have done with it.

That made me a number of enemies that I wasn't aware of. Enemies that took great joy at my downfall.

By this point my daily reinforcement videos were turning me into a different person. I no longer bemoaned cruel fate, I instead took a hard look at myself and decided I needed to know what I was doing that was garnering me more enemies than friends.

So I started reading and listening to books on psychology, especially those that focus on interaction with people.

I soon learned what I was doing wrong and took direct action to correct my behavior. And now I can safely say I have more friends than enemies and to those I wronged I tended a sincere apology.

Things are MUCH better now because I TOOK ACTION. I didn't realize that I was screwing up my life but once I did, I did something about it. And that is the key. Complaining changes nothing. You want your life to improve? DO THINGS that will make that improvement happen.

Don't get caught up in the 'Flavor of the Day"

When starting out anew many people make the mistake of getting caught up in the latest fad. If they are writers they start writing books on whatever is presently popular. If they open a store, they put in an order for whatever is selling the best right now. If they have a restaurant they buy the machinery that makes the latest fad food. The problem with this is that fads don't last. And usually by the time the writer finishes the book, the storeowner gets that shipment and the restaurateur installs that new specialty oven, those consumers have moved on to something else, and they are stuck with product with no buyers.

Successful people LEAD. They do not follow. They actively search for what is soon to be a major trend and focus their energies on how to capitalize on it.

Don't follow your bliss

I have no idea what hippie goof-ball came up with that touchy-feely life-lesson but it's a bad one. This is not to say that you shouldn't start a business doing what you like, it's that you must first find out if, by doing what you like, you will make money. I wrote a novel on how to make the book you wrote a best seller. The first thing I suggested they do was to type in the title of their book in Google's search box and see how many results they got.

If you type in Cowboys and Aliens you get over 3 million searches. If you type in, for example: The Heatlund Process you get 7.

Now the Heatlund Process could be a terrific book about Thomas Heatlund who discovered a remarkable new method that doubles a person's intelligence. But with 7 results who's going to know about it? If the author were to change the title to **Doubling your Intelligence: The Heatlund Process** however, the search results change from 7 to 81,000

Expect failure and disappointment.

I can tell you right now that you will fail and be disappointed on numerous occasions. There will be things that you will be sure will work for you and rocket you to the highest pinnacle of success.

And you will be greatly disappointed when they don't.

And it will happen again and again and again. It's at that point where most people revert to negative thinking and fall back into the failure techniques and ways that led to their unhappiness in the first place. And so, they give up and call books like this a crock.

But remember what Thomas Edison said: "I have not failed. I've just found 10,000 way that don't work."

Statistically 7 out of 10 businesses fail. Henry Ford filed for bankruptcy before becoming a success.

R.H Macy had several stores go out of business before his namesake business took off. Need I remind you of what George Washington went through? Did you see Mohammed Ali's fight against George Foreman?

If one method clearly isn't working out, try another. George Washington realized that he couldn't win without help, so he brought in a partner. The French. Henry Ford decided to focus on creating a specialty car. A single car that most people could afford to buy and use instead of trying to create many different models. Mohammed Ali realized he couldn't stay out of George's reach for 15 rounds so he changed his tactics and invented the 'Rope-a-dope."

If you are in a fist fight and someone punches you, it that it? Do you just give up? Take your ball and go home? No. You double your efforts and focus on ways to win. Make up your mind that somebody is going to fall and isn't going to be you. And when you win that fight there is no other feeling like it. It provides a tremendous burst of self-confidence and self-assuredness. And once you get your first win, you KNOW that you most certainly can get another.

Beware the bitter losers.

I mentioned earlier that I grew up in the Bronx, and although it wasn't all that great an environment, I received a superb education… And I don't mean the one from school.

What I learned is that many people, especially those who work menial jobs for low pay are very bitter about the way things turned out. Where was their lucky break, why didn't their ship come in? It wasn't fair. They were meant to be somebody, they were supposed to be a success. Somebody, somehow, someway, shafted them. Kept them from becoming the big deal they should have been, because their failure to succeed couldn't possibly be their own fault. And so they lie in wait, furious, and hell-bent on revenge.

And who do you think you are to come parading back here, showing off your fancy car and nice clothes!? Are you here to rub it in our faces!? Think you're better than us?! Huh? Well do ya?

Maybe someone ought to teach Mr. Fancy pants here a lesson!"

And that, my friend, is what I learned on the streets of the Bronx. Unsuccessful people don't applaud your good fortune, unsuccessful people aren't glad to see that you've done well. Unsuccessful people hate your stinking guts and will quickly turn on

you and take their failure and bitterness out on you.

Successful people on the other hand do applaud your success. They know from experience all the hard work it took to get you where you are. The long hours, the financial risks, the setbacks and false starts.

To think like a successful person you must adopt that attitude. You may not be lucky per se, and life may have knocked you around a lot more than the others BUT as mentioned earlier, there are ways around obstacles and you do that by accepting the hand you were dealt and start think of ways to win with it.

And how do you do this?

You bluff. You make your opponents think you have a better hand than you do. How many time have you seen a guy win at poker with absolutely nothing? I've certainly seen my share.

Which brings us back to the original premise. Dress, act and think like a successful person and people will believe you are and treat you like you are.

Become single-minded:

I am often amazed at the amount of people who sincerely believe that they are not smart enough or talented enough or simply good enough to become a success.

That's bad programming and it has to stop.

ANYONE can become a success. Over the course of my life I have learned (to my absolute astonishment) that simple minded people are often very successful.

And I think I have discovered why.

Simple minded people are also very *single* minded. They decide they want to do something and just start doing it. They don't clutter their mind with *"what ifs"* and possible mistakes that may happen or what people think. They have no imagination, no creativity and no delusions.

For example: John Doe decides that he likes cars and thinks he can make money selling them. So he gets a license to buy direct and rents a small lot on the side of a busy road. He puts up big signs saying Cars for Sale. He tells everyone he runs into that he sells cars. When he sees someone driving a crappy car at the mall or supermarket, he hands them his card. As he makes money he starts buying commercial time in which he shouts to the camera that he sells cars and you should buy one from

him. He creates as simple slogan. **Save Dough at John Doe's Cars!** There is nothing complex or unclear about his business plan. He doesn't care if people think he's pushy, or obnoxious. Doesn't care if his employees think he's a slave-driver or insensitive.

All he knows and cares about is that if he buys a car for $10,000 and sells it for $15,000 he has made $5,000.

John dropped out of school at 15. Today he is a millionaire.

So as you can see, becoming a success is simply a matter of deciding to do it. And yes there will be setbacks and pitfalls etc. But none of that matters because John didn't concern himself with what *might* happen. Didn't keep himself up nights worrying about *possible* failure. And when he encountered setbacks and pitfalls he simply shrugged, worked around them and continued selling cars.

Here's another reason why it's important to become a success especially if you're a man. Your wife expects it.

Oh they may tell you they'll love you forever whether you live in a palace or a shotgun shack but there is only so much sweating rent and food stamps and hand-me-downs they will put up with before they start looking around for greener pastures.

Remember they married you because they thought the two of you would have a wonderful life together. Sure it would be rough at first but over the years things would pick up and the money would start pouring in and the two of you would live happily ever after.

Well?

When looking for a mate, men want attractive women who are interesting and fun to be with. Women look for men who can protect them and provide a sense of security. Men they can be proud to be seen with, show off to their friends

When I did research for my divorce book, I discovered that the majority of the divorces that ended long term marriages were usually initiated by the wife and mostly because she felt she deserved more out of life than her husband was able to provide. So keep that in mind.

Where to start? Education is Key

We've discussed starting your life over but at what? Well, take some time to evaluate what you do best. Ask your friends what they think you're good at. Here's what I did. As a writer, I create and sell books. Over time I have learned the best ways to do this and the best way to make money doing it.

Then I realized that there must be many people who, like me, know how to do something that a lot of other people would like to know how to do. So I wrote the Best book on *How to Write Publish & Market*
Your Novel into a Bestseller
(http://www.amazon.com/Write-PublishMarket-Novel-
Bestsellerebook/dp/B00EHYIMCI/ref=sr_1_3?
s=digitaltext&ie=UTF8&qid=1389196887&sr=

13&keywords=zackary+richards then after publishing it I created an audio book version

Development/How-to-Write-Publish-and-Market-Your-Novel-into-a-Best-Seller-Audiobook/B00GUTI4FI/ref=a_search_c4_1_2_srTtl?qid=1389197027&sr=1-2 and a DVD version

http://www.amazon.com/How-Get-Your-BookPublished/dp/146755975X/ref=sr_1_1?ie=UTF8&_qid=1356651404&sr=8-1&keywords=Zackary+Richards+How+TO+GET+YOUR+BOOK+PUBLISHED

Then I created a Video Book trailer to promote it. http://www.youtube.com/watch?v=jB824cTL30&feature=youtu.be

It was while I was making the video book trailer that I realized there were a number of people probably doing the same thing with their skills. Making 'How-to' videos of their specialty. That when I decided it would be a good idea to set up a website that has collected a number of video tutorials that show and explain in great detail exactly how these skilled individuals perform their specialties.

There are many, many topics. For example: How to do HTML, How to open a restaurant, How to repair computers. How to become a pastry chef. How to open a Beauty Salon. How to do CSS programming. How to Type and dozens more. Here's the Link http://theundergroundcollege.com

So if you're looking for ideas, I suggest you start there. And consider this. The internet is the future, so ANY coding skills you acquire will automatically give you an advantage over those who don't.

And should you possess a particular skill that's in demand, you can add to your income by creating a video showing others what you know. You can learn exactly how to do this here:

https://www.udemy.com/how-to-create-an-awesomeonline-course/?affcode=E0EaeFtRTHQLQR53TA==

On the other hand say you have a good job with a good company and you want to start making your way up the corporate ladder. First, evaluate what you have to offer. What special skills or abilities do you possess that the company has need of? If you have nothing special to offer, then the company will likely have nothing to offer you.

Forget all the corporate mission plans and mission statements and that nonsense. The only thing you need to know is this: ***The most important person***

__in the company is the one that makes them the__
__most money.__

That person will survive every downsizing, every reorganization, every hostile take-over. He or she can be a complete ogre of a boss, a despicable human being and a complete failure as an executive but as long as he or she brings in the money, (or finds ways to save the company money) they can get away with just about anything.

You want to be that person. NOT the ogre, despicable human or executive failure of course but the person who brings in the MONEY! The Rainmaker!

So find out what skills you will need to become that person and do whatever is necessary to acquire them. Nearly anything can be learned on the internet or at distance learning classes like the ones listed at this organization.
http://learn.infiniteskills.com/

But enough about money for now. There will be a lot more on that later in the Finances section.

One of the most important aspects of this training is to show you how to make your life more fulfilling. To be able to go to bed each night and say "Wow! What a great day. I can't wait to see what tomorrow brings." Instead of, "Please God, get me out of this."

Like the old saying goes, "I've been rich & I've been poor. Rich is better." And so it stands to reason that, "I've been happy and I've been sad. Happy is better."

One of the best ways to acquire a sense of fulfillment is to help other's whose life has also been hit by Life's truck and are presently unable to get back on their feet. I am not suggesting you become a social worker (unless that's what you really want to do) because seeing and dealing that kind of misery day in and day out takes a very special type of person and likely not the type who is presently putting their own life back together.

That doesn't mean that you can't do something positive to help those down on their luck. Offer to volunteer at the local soup kitchen every so often and not just on holidays. People need assistance during the rest of the year and your time will be better served by being available when most needed.

Donate clothes that no longer fit. Furniture and other items you may no longer need. Remember that stuff from your old life we spoke about? The stuff that reminds you of all the horrors you went through? Well what's misery for you may be a blessing for someone else.

Next, start making new friends. And I don't mean network, business associates. I mean start making friends with people who have the same interests and likes that you do. People you can go with to a game or movie or engage in an activity with like motorcycle riding, bowling, tennis, softball, white water rafting, hiking, and so on.

But how do you meet these friends? Well, what do you like to do? Photography perhaps? Find a photography club in your area and join. Like softball or bowling? Look for the local teams and sign up. Like cooking? Join a cooking class.

The *New You* doesn't make excuses. The *New You* is a <u>doer</u> not a dreamer. The *New You* does not procrastinate.

The *New You* takes action now.

In order to be happy you need friends, activities that you enjoy and people to enjoy them with. The *New You* doesn't let things happen *to* you; he or she makes things happen *for* you.

It is very important that you make this a part of your life. When I started my new life I was amazed at all the opportunities I was offered by my new friends.

You see, everybody wants connections. Everybody wants to be part of something with like-minded people. So when my personal collapse hit, I joined a writers group. I enjoy writing, do it for a living and am happy to help others accomplish their writing goals. But what was most unexpected, was that by joining that writers group, a whole new section of life opened for me. I was invited to ride with a motorcycle group on a trek through the hills of Tennessee. Accompany a group of professional guider pilots, go white-water rafting, take part in a barbeque cook-off contest, Sail on a yacht, and a lot more. And it all happened because I decided to venture out of my comfort zone, meet new people and say yes to new experiences.

Never say to yourself, "I can't do that." Its defeatist and negative. If you've managed to learn reading, writing and arithmetic then there is no limit to what you can learn if you maintain a consistent "I CAN do that" attitude.

You've likely heard about creating a Bucket List. And if you haven't, it is a list of things you want to accomplish before you die. The problem is most people create that list, then put off doing or learning those things until it's too late.

Again, every time you dream about doing something you are wasting a portion of your life. Basically you're replacing an accomplishable reality with a time wasting fantasy.

And let me tell you something. No matter how great you imagine something to be, it doesn't come anywhere NEAR the actual experience itself. Skydiving just once, can change your life. Deep sea diving will show you things you never imagined existed. Learn to play a musical instrument and you can bring beauty with you wherever you go.

I was a musician for many years and for most of that time was in a band with a lead-singer (who I'll call Bob) who claimed he wanted to write songs but didn't know how to play guitar. I offered to teach him and promised that if he simply practiced for one-hour a day, every day, in six weeks he would be able to play guitar well enough to write any song his mind could imagine.

So he became very enthusiastic, bought a guitar, books on how to play, videos on techniques, the whole nine-yards. Claimed he was going to become a great guitarist and songwriter.

And he likely would have, except he failed to do one thing.

He didn't practice the one-hour a day for six weeks.

Oh he had a million excuses. Many of them were spectacular but so what? All he had to do was commit to practicing one lousy hour a day for six lousy weeks (which comes to a total of 42 hours which is just a little more than your average work week) and his dream would've come true. His goal would have been attained.

The guy was clearly talented but as Stephen King says, "Talent is a dime a dozen. Perseverance is far more valuable and far more likely to make you a success."

And here's the thing. If you do follow the instructions presented in this book you will notice small changes in your attitude and in your way of thinking. You'll find yourself having little patience with people like Bob and you'll start avoiding them. And you'll be annoyed by people who bemoan their circumstances yet make no concerted or prolonged effort to change them. Especially if you had to battle your way through hell itself to turn your own life around.

And this is why successful people want to be surrounded by other successful people, because successful people have accomplished things. They have found ways around problems, have shown that they are the type who doesn't stop when they are tired, they stop when they are finished.

Does that sound like you?

I know it hurts.

When I was down the last thing I wanted to hear was a lot of rah-rah, go get 'em champ, winners never quit and quitters never win, nonsense. I remember hearing some bible verse that says something like don't tale tales of joy to the suffering.

I understand. But I wrote this book because I have been where you are now and wished someone had told me that there was a way out of my circumstances and went on to SHOW me how, instead of quoting a bunch of pithy sayings and sanctimonious platitudes.

I didn't need a pep talk, a boot in the butt or a hand out.

I needed to be pointed in the right direction. I needed someone who had walked the walk and talked the talk to show me where I was failing and what I needed to do to rebuild the mess my life had become and permanently change it.

It took me seven long years. Seven years of trial and error (mostly error) before I was able to completely turn things around. And I had to learn the hard way. I wasn't aware of any book or video or seminar that could set me straight and show me the skills and attitude I would need to put my life back on track.

So I decided when I finally did turn things around I would write a book explaining to others who had found themselves in my former circumstances how to start over and rebuild their life.

Remember what Zig Ziglar said about what you needed to do to help accomplish your own goals? Well, what I did is what you are reading or listening to right now. I want you to do the following.

Take one of those notebooks you bought and write on the cover. *My Daily Accomplishments.*

And in that book I want you to write down exactly what you intend to accomplish. For example: Say you need a new job. Then update your resume and send it out to five companies that can use your particular abilities each day. Search for seminars that can update your skills. Subscribe to a newsletter specific to your discipline. Keep track of what you did and record the success rate. If sending out resumes isn't getting results, begin calling Human Resource departments and find out what they are presently looking for. If, for example, they need HTML programmers and are paying top dollar and you have some basic programming skills then take an HTML course and let them know you're available and have what they're looking for.

In the end all it really boils down to is the person who succeeds is the person who took the time to find out what was needed and found a way to provide that service.

As I wrap up this section I want to introduce you to the person who is likely the one responsible for all your present misfortunes. He or she is the one who has kept you from achieving the things you set out to do, is likely the one that screwed up your personal life and the one behind your financial downfall.

That person's name?

Your ***EGO***

Let me first say that I know from which I speak. I was blessed with a number of talents that have permitted me to do things most people can't. This isn't bragging because I had nothing to do with the creation of these abilities. I was simply born with them.

Now you would think that because I was so blessed, that good luck would accompany it. And maybe it did, but my enormous ego prevented me from seeing or taking advantage of it.

If you happened to be born with a lot of talent, spending your formative years in the Bronx is not a good idea. Many of its residents (but certainly not all) are descended from bitter, angry people whose lives are one of unrelenting misery. They are unlucky, unhappy and bitterly envious and jealous of anyone's success or good fortune. As John Lennon once sang: *They hate you if you're clever and they despise a fool.*

Despite all my talents I wasn't intuitive enough to realize that showing them all the things I could do (that they couldn't) wasn't entertaining them.

To them I was showing off. To them I was saying, *"Look at how much better I am than you! Look at all the great things I can do that you can't."* Needless to say, I spent a good deal of my childhood fighting. But did I stop showing off? With all this so-called talent you'd think I'd realize that I was in an urban jungle and like in the real jungle, the pack always kills the one that is different.

Like the Japanese say. *__The nail that sticks up is the one beaten down.__*

You likely have no idea just **how much** your ego has screwed up your life. Remember that pretty girl you wanted to ask out but didn't, because if she refused your ego would have been crushed? That team you wanted to try out for but didn't because your ego was afraid you'd look like a fool? That argument you had with someone who you really cared about but you couldn't apologize because your ego simply wouldn't let you. That incredibly stupid thing you said, simply because your feathers got ruffled and your ego demanded you lash out. Or that person you slept with when you were in a committed relationship because your ego convinced you that you deserved 'something on the side.' Or that excellent advice a successful professional in your selected field gave you that you took as an insult, because your ego convinced you that you didn't need their help.

Then there was that investment you made. Friends and family warned you that it was a bad idea, even showed you documentation why it wouldn't work. But you did it anyway, because your ego wouldn't let you back down because it convinced you that you could.

So as it turns out the cause of our own misfortunes is often ourselves. Sometimes we are our own worst enemies. But some of the blame must be shared with the media because they constantly present stories about a singular person overcoming enormous odds. And I will say this yet again. Those instances are the exception NOT the rule. A singular person going up against enormous odds ***Will Fail*** and be horribly crushed 99 times out of a hundred. Most revolutions don't succeed and the participants are routinely executed.

Don't allow yourself to be drugged with happy ending stories that are often the result of a freak accident or an insanely lucky break. Never forget that inventive and properly executed plays win far more football games that any last minute Hail Mary pass.

So since you are committing yourself to starting over, the one, and probably most important thing you should set out to do is to stop letting your ego control your actions. And that's REALLY hard. But it can be done and done through a method I hate. I hate it because it's difficult to do, but it does work.

It's called *Desensitization Therapy.*

In desensitization therapy you purposefully do the things your ego tries to prevent you from doing. Force yourself to talk to that person you're attracted to. Ask for that raise from your boss or advice from someone who is more successful than you are.

Remember the worst they can do is say no.

And the only thing that can be hurt is your ego. Nothing else. A refusal will not land you on the ground bleeding and in need emergency care. You will not require rehabilitation and therapy. You will not be scarred for life (unless you have some form of mental illness.) But… and this is important to remember. Sometimes they say *yes*! And with every yes, your life gets a little better. So make up your mind to override your ego every time it objects. Learn to give it no say in your decisions and your life will become much better for it.

Section Two: Rebuilding Your Body

To begin I must point out that I am not a licensed physician, nor am I a nutritionist, herbologist or healthcare professional. It is always advisable to talk with your doctor regarding any change in your diet or exercise regimen. There may be factors involved that may make some of these suggestions a health risk so first make sure you're good to go.

What I will present in this section are various foods and techniques that I have personally used to rebuild my health after I spend a considerable amount of time feeling sorry for myself and letting myself go to seed.

It's a common reaction when all seems lost.

Shortly after our lives become a donkey ride through hell, we often fall into depression and just let everything go. We don't care what happens emotionally, physically or financially. We're in a deep funk and have no idea on where to start to turn things around.

I get that.

But now that you're reading this book you've obviously come back far enough to consider having a look at getting yourself back into shape.

Let me point out that I am not a health aficionado. I don't run marathons, lift weights, jog, cleanse, juice or start my day by dunking my head into a bucket of ice water.

But I am remarkably healthy (knock wood) but I had to make a number of changes in the way I ate and looked at food in order to make that happen.

When my former life disintegrated, I ate crappy fast food because I didn't want to go home. Drank more beer than I should have and spent all my free time sitting in a chair writing and smoking.

Needless to say I became fat, out of shape and considerably unhealthy. I developed a rasping cough, ran out of breath climbing stairs, and couldn't sleep. Had chronic acid reflux and ate TUMS like candy. Developed chronic anxiety, heart palpitations, ulcers and edema.

Sound familiar?

Then astoundingly, I got lucky!

I didn't know how lucky at first. In fact, while luck was trying to get my attention, I was probably stuffing my face with crap and muttering about how unfair life was.

But the TV was on and in the background some guy was blathering about health, rebuilding your immune system and making yourself feel twenty years younger.

I continued to ignore him because I've heard that sales pitch before and every diet I've been on only lasts for so long and then I start putting on the pounds. So I went back to reading the paper or whatever but then he said something I had never heard before in any infomercial.

He said the reason people overeat yet are constantly hungry is because we're not eating the foods our bodies need to function properly. Each day our bodies need certain nutrients and foods rich in vitamins to do what it needs to do and when it doesn't get those nutrients and vitamins it sends out a hungry signal.

So we eat and eat and are still hungry. Why?

Because we aren't eating the *right* things. If we ate the right things, the infomercial guy said, the hunger signals would stop and we would naturally begin to lose weight because we wouldn't be hungry.

Wait. That actually made sense.

Okay, the guy got my attention. So I put down whatever I was doing and listened. Turns out the speaker was Dr. Joel Fuhrman, a board certified medical doctor who specializes in food and nutrition. He claimed that the medical profession and pharmaceutical companies aren't interested in helping you get well. They make their make money by addressing symptoms not curing illnesses.

Because they don't make any money from healthy people.

He went on to cite numerous cases where people suffering from serious heart disease made a complete recovery, lowered their blood pressure, cured acid reflux, cured edema, and restored vitality and drive by simply changing their diet.

And all you had to do to accomplish this was to eat the right foods, every day. If you did you wouldn't be hungry, your body's ills would repair themselves, your energy levels would increase and your mental attitude would improve.

I was unconvinced, but Dr. Fuhrman continued to present documented evidence and testimonials from before and after cases. I still wasn't convinced but what he did say made sense. The key, he said again was to eat the foods your body needs every day to function properly and he went so far to say exactly what they were.

He called it the GOMBS diet. GOMBS is actually an acronym for the following foods: **Greens-Onions-Mushrooms-Berries and Seeds/nuts.** And they don't have to be eaten all at once. For example I have a bowl of blueberries with a teaspoon of flax seeds on them (with whipped cream) for breakfast. Have onions on my afternoon burger and for dinner have string beans & mushroom chicken. You can mix it up any way you like. Put the mushrooms on your burger and have onions with your greens. Eat nuts and raisins as a snack. As long as you eat some combination of all 5 **each day** you will likely see marked improvement.

For my own testimonial, when I bought Dr. Fuhrman's book *Eat to Live* and started following his suggested diet plan (Note* he suggests you switch to an all veggie diet, which I won't do, but it still works if you continue to eat burgers and pasta.)

And here's the most amazing thing. He was absolutely right about the food cravings. Once I started eating the GOMBS each day I discovered my appetite decreased significantly. After a strawberry yogurt with flax seeds mixed in for breakfast I found I wasn't hungry again until dinner time. And come dinner time I found myself eating smaller portions.

Then the acid reflux cleared up. Where I used to live on Zantac and Tums, within a few weeks I had no need for them at all. Then the weight started dropping off. Within 4 months I lost nearly thirty pounds!

Also during that time the swelling in my fingers and ankles went down, my energy levels went up and I started feeling good both mentally and physically. And what's more it made me healthy enough to again enjoy my unhealthy pleasures like pizza, tacos and chicken wings.

Will it cure all your health problems? I have no idea but it did wonders for me and there is sound science to back it up. *NEVERTHELESS, always consult your healthcare professional before beginning any health related regimen.*

Bottom line? Unless you have some condition that would prevent you from using this method (a nut allergy for example) it will likely benefit you.

So the book is called *Eat to Live* by Dr. Joel Fuhrman M.D. If you're having health issues you might want to pick up a copy.

Visit an acupuncturist.

As you've likely noticed I'm not much for happy thoughts and good intentions to make things all better. I am a pragmatist to the point where I only believe something works when I have personally experienced its benefits.

I don't believe in crystals, or chanting or vegetarianism or any of that jazz, I just believe in me. Yoko and me, that's reality. However, I've become quite a fan of acupuncture and the people who are certified to practice it.

Here's what happened.

One day out of the blue my left thigh began to hurt. I thought nothing of it at first but with each following day the pain grew worse, So much so it got to the point where I could hardly walk.

So I went to the doctor who, after considerable effort and thought, diagnosed my condition as "Beats the hell out of me" and prescribed steroids, anti-inflamatories and pain killers.

I'm not crazy about taking any medication but with the pain increasing each day I buckled under and took the meds as prescribed.

But they didn't work. The pain-killers killed the pain somewhat but the condition wasn't getting better. A week later I'm in the emergency room and in excruciating pain. The doctor orders x-rays. The x-rays show no damage or tumors. In fact to the eye the leg seems just fine. The doctor confirms the original diagnosis except he refers to it as "CHRONIC beats the hell out of me" and loads me up with more pain killers and schedules a MRI

It's then I notice that I'm getting that, *It's all in your head* kind of look you get when the Doctor has no idea how to fix you.

I run this by my daughter, who studied medicine in college. The next thing I know I have an appointment with an acupuncturist.

I'm in pain and not at all enthusiastic. To which my daughter reminds me that the doctor clearly had no idea of how to cure my condition, so the next step was to try an alternative venue.

So I went and the acupuncturist was an attractive woman in her mid-thirties with an extensive background in biology. During the procedure she asked a number of questions about my diet and daily routines. When finished she said my condition sounded like a magnesium deficiency and that I should purchase magnesium in powdered form and have a teaspoonful each day in water and to take a dropperful of B vitamins as well.

I was very impressed with her knowledge of how the body worked so I did as she said and within three days the pain had subsided significantly, within ten days it was gone.

I still take the magnesium each day because when I miss a few days the pain starts in again so she obviously knew what she was talking about.

The acupuncture sessions also helped untie the knot I had tightened myself into and brought about some much needed clarity to my thinking. My frustrations had led to a short fuse and anger issues. And I later learned this can lead to serious heart problems. So I'm glad I tried something that is often referred to as faux-science because it not only helped me over a health problem it also lowered my blood pressure.

Although I have no idea how it works I do recommend it. It doesn't hurt at all and you'll likely feel considerably better after the first few sessions.

Exercise:

As mentioned earlier, I'm no fan. But as you age certain realities must be acknowledged if you don't want 'Health Issues' to be added to the other problems you're presently trying to scrape off your plate.

Another reason is as you lose weight you'll notice sagging skin that makes you feel unattractive and self-conscientious. So you're going to need to exercise to tighten things up. Many health books suggest you take up activities like tennis, bike riding or hiking.

The area where I live has an extended winter season, so things like tennis, bike riding and hiking are only possible during a select part of the year. But I had to do something because I was on a roll by this point. I was watching the positive reinforcement videos each morning, I did one thing each day that my ego tried to keep me from doing, I was following Dr. Fuhrman's diet plan (for the most part) and had a less stress and could sleep better largely due to the acupuncture.

So the sagging skin had to go.

Since I couldn't go the activities route I decided to purchase a skiing machine. One of those gizmo's that makes it possible to exercise both your arms and legs at the same time. So I set it up in my office, and following the instructions, proceeded to give it a try.

Let me just say it wasn't as easy as the people on TV made it look. Also I was in worse shape than I thought because after three minutes I was huffing and puffing like a beached walrus.

So for the first week I only managed 3 minutes a day. Come week two, I managed to up the daily drill to 5 minutes.

Then things started to pick up. The next week I cracked the ten minute mark and 3 days after that made it to a half hour.

I figured that a half hour a day was a reasonable amount of exercise but after a couple of weeks the routine became boring and I was losing interest. While cleaning things out of the house I came upon one of my daughter's dance CD's and remembered her and her friends blaring the music and wildly dancing in her room.

So I decided to see if while exercising I could keep up with the music.

It was a much larger challenge than I thought. Those dances song really moved! None of that easy listening, take it slow, mon, Reggae music. NO! This stuff was created to get you up and get you moving. One after the other, no let up.

Seven minutes in, I was sweating so much it looked like I had just come in out of the rain. By the end of the second song I was done! So I set a new goal. Each day I would exercise to this dance CD and would keep at it until I was able to keep up with each song and continue all the way through until I was able to make it to the end of the CD.

Admittedly it took a while but I did do it. And not only was the sagging skinned middle-aged body gone. It had been replaced by that of a fairly buff guy easily ten years younger than I actually was.

I hope I'm making it clear that what happened to me was no quick fix. The physical turn around took months. But I wasn't looking at the clock. I had adopted the attitude of not stopping when I was tired, I only stopped when I was done.

As mentioned in the beginning, starting over isn't easy. It takes commitment, drive and perseverance.

There will be days when nothing goes right, when it looks like you're aren't making any progress, when all your hard work simply isn't paying off.

But if there are little advancements, nothing major, just little advancements then you MUST stick with it because as the saying goes, the journey of a thousand miles begins with a single step. And never forget that by giving up, your old life will return and you'll be right back to where you started.

And MOST importantly, ***always keep in mind that you are taking action.*** You are living, you are swinging for the fences every time at bat. It is said that fortune favors the brave. Well guess what? **YOU Are Brave!** And should you believe in a God and an afterlife, when asked what you did with the life you got you can safely answer, "I gave it everything I had!"

And that is a satisfactory answer.

How to Quit Smoking Once and For All!

This will be hard. Probably one of the hardest thing you will ever do. You need to truly understand that going in because one of the reasons many people fail is they don't fully comprehend what an enormous task this is.

I do.

I started smoking at age 15 and continued for decades.

This is not something I am proud of. But I'm not ashamed of it either. When I started smoking I really didn't know what I was getting into. Smoking was on TV all the time. Lucy & Desi smoked continuously (Desi died of lung cancer) Humphrey Bogart always had a cigarette in his mouth in the old movies (also died of lung cancer) as did The Twilight Zone's Rod Serling (died of heart disease).

All the Beatles smoked as did the Rolling Stones. The Rat Pack smoked, John Wayne smoked (also died of lung cancer)

All the cool guys and girls smoked.

So I smoked.

And once I had a two pack a day habit the results started rolling in. Empirical evidence that smoking did indeed cause lung cancer AND heart disease. They began putting warning labels on. Started antismoking commercials. Cigarette smoking was banned from television commercials, shortly afterward TV scenes showing people smoking was banned too.

Smoking became a pariah and anyone who smoked was looked upon with distain.

But the really cool people still smoked so who cares what those goody two-shoes thought? Then George Harrison died of throat cancer.

Over the many years I smoked I did attempt to stop a number of times, but always went back. One time I had stopped for nearly three years and still went back.

But those failures weren't a complete disaster because I eventually learned what method DID work and what I had to do to make sure I stopped smoking permanently.

There are a number of ways that are successful at first and appear to really work. Unfortunately within six months the overwhelming majority are back puffing away, vowing that the next time they will stop for good.

Except they don't. And as a result they feel helpless and weak. They start beating themselves up and fall into that trap of believing that they are losers that can't succeed.

And that is a slippery slope, people.

So, if you smoke here's how you're going to stop, once and for all.

The most important factor I hammered in again and again in the previous section is that in order to succeed, you MUST convince yourself that you CAN do it. Giving it a try, giving it a whirl, taking a shot at it is a waste of time and money.

In order to quit smoking YOU MUST MAKE UP YOUR MIND THAT YOU WILL NEVER SMOKE AGAIN.

And that is step #1 and so I will repeat it YOU MUST MAKE UP YOUR MIND THAT YOU WILL NEVER SMOKE AGAIN.

It doesn't matter that you're having a hard time at work. It doesn't matter that you are having a hard time with your relationship, it doesn't matter if someone dies, it doesn't matter FILL IN THE BLANK. Because there is no reason valid enough for you to start smoking once you stop.

NONE!!

Why? Because regardless of what terrible thing is occurring in your life, smoking won't fix it. Smoking won't make it better, smoking won't make your problems go away.

But smoking will very likely kill you.

But you know that and keep smoking anyway because you're hooked and it has become such an intricate part of your life that you are unsure of what effect stopping smoking might have on you.

Back when I smoked I'd go through two packs a day while writing a book. I believed that smoking kept me sharp, jump-started my creativity, cleared my mind. And I was concerned that should I stop, I might not be able to write.

Plus I believed there were definite advantages to smoking. When I worked in corporate I got to know most of my co-workers when we all went out for a smoke. One of the best ways to strike up a conversation was to offer someone a cigarette.

That's how I met the woman who would become my wife.

But the sober realities were becoming more and more difficult to ignore. One by one the people I knew stopped smoking. And the one's that didn't started having health problems. A woman I worked with for seven years and one I smoked with everyday developed cancer and died within the year. Another co-worker I smoked with developed heart problems and was only in his mid-forties. And I still smoked.

Then one day I decided it was time to stop. My wife and I had just bought a new house and she had quit two years earlier. She never complained about my smoking but I felt the time had come for me to stop.

Period.

Because I had failed a number of times before, I knew what was ahead. I knew how difficult it would be and what I needed to do to make sure I didn't relapse.

First, I made up my mind that this time I would stop permanently. There would be no relapses, no excuses, no trying my best. Once I stopped I was NEVER GOING TO SMOKE AGAIN.

I haven't had a cigarette (or cigar or pipe or whatever) in twelve years. And remember, I was a two pack a day guy. Not one of those who can smoke one or two cigarettes and then not have another for a few days. Basically if you saw me I likely had a cigarette in my hand. So don't go telling yourself that smoking for you will be harder because you smoked more. The withdrawal from stopping smoking two packs a day is the same as stopping smoking four packs a day.

Remember this method is useless if you haven't make up your mind to stop. Any half-hearted attempt WILL end in failure.

So, here's what you need to do. Make a list of at least ten reasons why you ARE stopping smoking. Too often, like looking back on a bad relationship, you only remember the good times. You need to remind yourself regularly why this needs to be done. Write those reasons on the back of a business card and keep in next to your credit cards. This way those reasons will always be in reach when you begin having doubts (and you will).

Next step get rid of EVERY ITEM associated with smoking. EVERY ashtray, EVERY lighter, even the expensive ones you received as a gift or was handed down by a relative. (If they loved you they would want you to get rid of something that will likely help kill you.)

Next, tell everyone you know you are quitting. EVERYONE. Tell them you will likely be difficult and short tempered. Ask for their help, ask them not to invite you out for a smoke. Ask them not to mention cigarettes and to please keep them out of your sight. If you need more incentive, tell them if you _**ever**_ start smoking again you will personally pay each of them $50 cash. (More if you happen to make real money)

Next buy several boxes of Nicorette gum. Not one, not two, several like six or seven. Then open the boxes, separate the strips and place a strip in every coat and jacket, in every pair of pants, In the kitchen drawer, in the glove compartment of your car, in your desk at the office, in your spouse's car, in your teen's car. In your friends car. In your wallet, in every purse you own. Place a strip in every vehicle you might drive, motorcycle, boat, truck, minivan. Keep a strip in the fridge. And every other place you can think of.

And here's why.

Cravings hit you like a punch in the head. BOOM! You want a cigarette and you want one NOW! If you have a piece of Nicorette gum available at that very moment you will likely reach for the gum and muscle through the craving.

If you don't, every minute you have to deal with that craving without relief the more likely you will succumb and buy a pack of cigarettes.

Then you will be a disappointment not only to yourself but to everyone who went out of their way to support you in your efforts to quit smoking. You will have to come up with the money to pay off the wager and STILL be stuck buying cigarettes every day.

Here's another event that will likely cause you to start smoking again.

You try the patch or Chantix to quit smoking. It works fine and makes it much easier to stop smoking than Nicorette gum.

But here's the problem. Both the patch and Chantix need time to start working. So let's say you use the patch or Chantix for say six weeks. Then lower the dosage and stop using altogether. You do great for six months then

BOOM! The cravings hit and hit hard! But...but... you haven't had a cigarette in six months! How could you possibly have cravings after such a long time??!

I'll tell you why. But first let me explain that this was told to me by someone who had successfully quit smoking and said this was the reason the cravings returned. I don't have any medical evidence to back this up but as a reason why the cravings come back after months and sometimes years, I find it very believable.

The gentlemen explained why cravings suddenly return after months and years after stopping smoking is because tiny packets of nicotine remain in the bloodstream for as long as five years and when one of them bursts, the body recognizes it, want more of it and sends a full blast craving alert to the brain. Often stronger than any previous craving because it's been so long and the body really, really, really wants its nicotine fix.

I know, because as mentioned earlier, I once stopped smoking for nearly three years then out of nowhere an immense craving hit me and that was that. I didn't have any Nicorette gum available so I started smoking again and continued for another seven years.

This is a fact. It takes five years to successfully quit smoking. You should never say you have quit smoking unless you haven't smoked in five years.

When I did successfully quit. I had packets of Nicorette gum EVERYWHERE for five straight years. And since I knew the cravings could hit me at any time during the five years I kept on my guard. To this day, twelve years since my last smoke, I still occasionally find Nicorette gum packets in the back of my closet, in an old gym bag. In an old suitcase, and somewhere down the line I'll likely find more. But that's fine. Because every time I do, I smile because I did it! I quit smoking!

And I should note I didn't have a single craving following the first five years. And I'm quite sure I'll never have one again because the concept of drawing smoke into my lungs willingly is something I'm never going to do again.

So that, my friend is exactly how to quit smoking. I know some people who have quit smoking with the patch and with Chantix and electronic cigarettes BUT, if you are a heavy smoker like I was, I strongly doubt they will work over the long run. The advantage of the gum is that you take a bite or two then keep it in between your check and gum until all the nicotine is absorbed.

It is in no way as satisfying as having a cigarette, but it does take the edge off enough to outlast the craving. (Most craving last between 7 to 10 minutes) although when you're going through it, it seems considerably longer!) Plus you only take it when you need it, unlike Chantix and the patch whose chemicals are always in your blood stream weather you need them or not.

To wrap up this chapter I would like to once more stress the importance of putting the time and effort to clear your mind of unnecessary crap, (you really don't need to know who the next reality show winner is going to be, or what family of shameless imbeciles will melt down next) and to make sure your body gets the proper nutrients and vitamins it needs to run smoothly. Remember ***what you put*** _**into your brain and your body is what you become.**_

FINANCES, Past, Present & Future

As Bob Dylan once sang, ***"You don't need to be a weather man to know which way the wind blows."*** So I'm here to tell you the winds of change are coming.

And they're not bringing good news.

First, let me point out that I'm not trying to sell you anything (other than this book of course) so please keep that in mind as you read this section because it will likely cause you some concern.

For those of you unfamiliar with my blog zackaryrichards.blogspot.com you should know that for the last few years I have been writing on how the financial meltdown of 2008 brought about a massive change in the way America does business, and most people are not aware of how that change with deeply affect them and their future.

Simply put, the human employee is being phased out. Don't agree? Well then why is the stock market at its highest peak ever while unemployment continues to be a major problem?

Oh they tell you things are picking up but do you believe what you hear or what you see? The government employment figure are routinely skewed to give the indication that companies are hiring again, that manufacturing is picking up, & jobs are returning to the private sector.

Have you seen any evidence of that? I haven't. In my area a G.E. plant recently closed and Global Foundries, a major chip manufacturer is scheduling lay-offs. What's more I continue to see small businesses closing shop because they can't compete with the ever growing Big Box stores that pay minimum wage and provide no benefits. And it's those jobs, the minimum wage jobs that the government is exploiting as the new employment growth and the economic comeback. You know as well as I that you can't feed a family with a minimum wage job, and you can barely make ends meet if you have two of them. The distance between the haves and the have-nots is steadily increasing.

So let's address the realities and what it means for you especially if you're young and are looking to find a good job and prosper financially.

During my father's day (back in the 1950s) the American worker was at its prime. Dad went to work, mom stayed home and the bills were paid.

During my generation, (the 1980s) both Mom and Dad worked, life was hectic, kids were shuttled around, day care came into existence and bills got paid.

During my children's generation (the 2010s) they took on staggering debt to get the education needed for good paying job, then discovered those jobs had been outsourced, leaving them with few opportunities and staggering debt.

Many economists are saying that the jobs will come back once the emerging nations' work force economy grows to the point where they are being paid the same as American Workers. And they refer to Japan's economic growth spurt during the 1970's which has long since leveled off.

And sadly people say, *"Well that makes sense. We just have to stick it out until things pick up."*

If the government believed that things would pick up they wouldn't have purchased two billion rounds of ammunition and armored vehicles, would they? Ever notice that during times of prosperity there aren't riots, or protests or random violence?

And why should there be? If you're paying your bills and are able to sock away a few bucks each week you're not going to riot or protest. Things are good so sit back and enjoy it.

So let me present this fact. This coming economic future is inevitable, things AREN'T going to get better for the middle class, the stock market will continue to rise and lay-offs will increase. Corporate CEOs will make more money than ever as the middle-class worker is driven into poverty.

In this section, I'm going to show you how to keep these changes from driving you into the streets and to actually **prosper** using the same tactics big businesses are presently using to phase workers out.

But before I continue, I must point out that this bleak future neither the government's or businesses fault (at least not completely.) The culprit responsible is our rapidly emerging technology.

And I'm not talking about gadgets, or cell phones or tablets although they do have a part in it. What really brought about this new economy is the internet, in particular, internet shopping.

Amazon, once a fledgling on-line tech company has become one of the biggest, and most profitable companies in existence. In addition it has been rated the #1 company in customer service for nine straight years. And while companies like Sears and

K-Mart struggle to stay in business, Amazon's profits are growing in leaps and bounds.

Why? Because Amazon has no brick and mortar stores with the overhead costs that go with them. No salespeople, no display models, no cleaning crews, no window dressers. No holiday decorations, no ASCAP costs, no slippery floors that generate lawsuits, I could go on but you get the picture.

The point is they have very few employees considering the enormous size of their business.

In addition, customers don't have to weather the elements to purchase the products they sell, and with today's HD televisions and computer monitors, the clarity of the product image is almost as sharp is seeing the product live and up close. Their return policy is very liberal, if you don't like it, send it back and they'll return your money.

What's more, there are no lines, no crowds, no closing time, no opening time, no school organizations at the entrances hitting you up for donations, no sneezing children passing their germs on to you, instead they are there 24 hours a day, seven days a week ready to serve your every shopping desire.

That my friend, is the future.

With the costs of power rising every years, people will need to cut back on every device that requires money to run it. Why put gas in the car and drive miles to the nearest big-box store only to discover that they don't have what you're looking for? Why not simply go on line, select what you want, get it at a lower price, *plus* save the money that would have been spent for gas?

Why not indeed?

As a writer I love book stores. Alas, they're a dying breed. With Amazon providing electronic versions of the same book at a fraction of the cost. Your only reason to buy the hard cover is that you enjoy paying more to lug around a four or five pound novel.

Reality is this. People are pragmatic. They go into a mom & pop book store and come across a book they like, but instead of buying it there, they go home, get online, go to Amazon and order an e-book version at a far lower price or order a hard cover used version at again, a far lower price.

Another hard reality is that physical books are also on the way out. Every time gas prices go up so does the price of ink. So do shipping costs. To save money book editors are being replaced by software programs which is why many new books are filled with grammatical and spelling mistakes.

Times are tough, people are doing all they can to save money.

Computer tablets are becoming better, faster, more advanced and are providing more services with each new roll out. They are getting lighter, have illuminated screens, and can jump right on the net should you become deeply engrossed in a serial novel and simply must have to next book in the series right now!

Which brings us to libraries. I love libraries! There are few things I like more than spending a cold February Saturday afternoon in my local library, with a cup of hot cocoa, a good book and a comfortable chair by the window with the fireplace warming my chilled bones, (and yes my local library has all of these.)

Unfortunately they'll all be gone soon, too. Will probably be outlawed. Think about it. Libraries are big buildings that require light, heat and power. They don't generate any income and are expensive to run.

So in order to cut costs, libraries will be forced to put all their books on computer, to be downloaded instead of borrowed. And that's where the problems arise. Big corporations aren't going to allow libraries to give away electronic versions of the very novels they are selling online and will strongly petition the government to put an end to it.

And so bye-bye libraries. I'll miss you so much.

Now let's talk about those outsourced customer service jobs that will be coming back once the emerging nations' economies price themselves out of the market.

It's not going to happen.

And it's not because those emerging nations won't price themselves out of the market, what I mean is that they are going to lose those customer service jobs too!

"But who are they going to lose them to?" you ask.

It's not a **_who_** it's a **_what._**

Ladies and gentlemen let me introduce you to the future of customer service. Its name is Watson and it's a specialty computer created by IBM.

To give you an idea of Watsons's capabilities, the TV show Jeopardy held a contest between its two winningest players and Watson in a three day competition.

Watson won.

Which means that one single computer was able to answer correctly more questions than Jeopardy's two best players, Ken Jennings and Brad Rutter.

A big deal was made of that event and Jennings's comment **"I for one, welcome our new computer overlords."** got a lot of airplay.

Unfortunately, that comment is slowly becoming a reality.

As for Watson, do you actually think IBM spent millions of dollars and thousands of man hours just to create a product that could beat Jeopardy's best players?

That IS what they wanted us to think.

What Watson was actually created to do was to replace all customer service workers in all companies in all countries. It's not quite ready to step into that role just yet, but say within five years, if you're still working in customer service, you won't be in six.

You see, with Watson having beaten Jeopardy's best players, IBM proved that their one machine could do a better job answering customer questions than any number of customer service reps. Plus it requires no days off, no healthcare, no insurance, no sick days, no vacations, no pregnancy leave, & no childcare. It works 24/7 and is never wrong and is incapable of human errors.

So what jobs are safe? Well we'll always need doctors.

Are you sure? MRI's give such detailed accounts of what's inside the human body that new software programs could easily diagnose the problem, likely more accurately than a doctor and, like Watson, have instant access to the most successful methods in treating that condition. Surgeons? We already have robotic surgeons in the operating rooms right now, doing very complex procedures like cancer removal.

What about Accountants?

I assume you've heard of Turbo-tax and QuickBooks? Each year more people are using that program to file their taxes, and like the other software programs, they are incapable of human error.

How about Travel agents?

What's a travel agent?

Heard of the Google car? It's a car that's driven entirely by computer. Fascinating to watch, even more fascinating when you stop and realize that this technology is being developed to replace truck drivers and other service haulers.

Because once again, computers don't need anything other than electricity, they can run 24/7 and don't need to hit the rest stop. Which mean truck stops will be a thing of the past. As well as the jobs they provide.

And speaking of things in the past I noticed that the nearby Walmart increased the number of their self-serve check out aisles from four to twelve. And if you're one of those people who are concerned about the poverty wages paid by companies like Walmart and McDonalds to their employees, you needn't worry.

The Big Boxes will adopt the Amazon business plan and close their brick & mortar stores. So that will be that for the Walmart employee.

As for the McDonalds workers, well. They are going to be jettisoned as well. In California a new business called Burrito Box is selling freshly made Mexican food from a vending machine. But this isn't new, vending machines that provide hot & ready specialty foods are popping up all over the world, so get ready for a mechanical voice asking if "You want fries with that?"

Math is math. Business will ALWAYS chose the most profitable business plan. And as bleak as that news sounds it's a lot worse. Why? Because there is a relatively new product whose technology is advancing at an amazing rate and one many venture capitalists are investing heavily in.

And what is that product?

It is called the 3D printer.

And that, my friend is the name of our new computer overlord. Just as the computer became the main driver of business in the eighties & nineties, the 3D Printer will have an even bigger effect on the 21st century.

You can see a number of videos on YouTube demonstrating how 3D printers work but to give you an overview, what it does is create a three dimensional model of the blueprint you scan into its computer. Need an adjustable wrench? Scan the blueprint and it will make an exact duplicate, and not only a duplicate, a duplicate that can do everything an actual adjustable wrench can do.

Take moment to think of all the applications for such a device. It is, in effect an assembly line team in itself. With its present technology it can duplicate anything in plastic, many things in ceramics, glass, synthetic materials, chemicals, metals and in some cases even food.

It is already being used to construct modular homes, guitars, clothing, artificial limbs, car parts, toys, computer parts, furniture, human organs and much, much more and all without any assistance from people. And what's even more unsettling is that they ***can replicate themselves!***

So you're probably asking yourself, "Where is my place in this future?"

That's a question you need to start figuring out an answer to.

Or you can consider my plan.

Before the industrial revolution of the late 1800 we were a mostly agrarian society. We raised crops and sold them at market. We created products and sold them to those who needed it.

In those days we were mostly entrepreneurs. Although entrepreneurship wasn't viewed with the esteem it is viewed with today. Back then it was called *find something to sell or starve.*

But the thing is, we did. And more importantly, the community we lived in was far more important than it is now. Trade between communities is what kept them alive.

In today's world, with the internet and Facebook we have business associates and friends whom we've never met in person. For example, I'm good friends with a woman who I met on the internet. I don't know her real name, where she lives or what she looks like. Yet, I enjoy emailing her and comparing notes regarding our writing careers.

Life has changed but some things stay the same. When corporate jobs dry up, we will have to revert to the old ways. And that is doing business and trading within our communities, but not only our physical communities, we'll be trading with our INTERNET COMMUNITIES.

As a publisher and a writer I make my money selling my products and services over the internet. Like any business it took time to build and I had my share of setbacks along the way. Certain ventures didn't pan out. I invested in products that promised much but did little. And sadly ran into some outright crooks but fortunately no more than you would meet in normal life.

But I ALSO met and learned from some amazing and talented individuals who were very knowledgeable, helpful and extremely generous with their time. It was those people who showed me how to get to where I am today.

You see, I don't need a corporate job. I don't need to get up at some ungodly hour and drive to some remote location to perform assigned tasks for eight hours.

I get up when I please, work as much or as little as I deem necessary, do work I enjoy, discuss book projects with talented and engaging professional men and women and spend time devising ways to increase my income by utilizing specific sub genres of my niche, publishing. And by providing tutorials for people looking to find a way to improve their lives, learn a marketable skill, start a business and do all that at a reasonable price.

But that's my thing.

What do you need to do now to ensure you're not obsolete within the next few years?

You need to learn how to make money on the internet.

The internet provides a world market, it provides potential customers from every online country.

The possibilities of profit are far larger than you can possibly imagine. And **_NOW_** is the time to start learning **_HOW_** because the longer you wait the bigger your competition is going to be.

"But I have no idea on how to start!" you say.

No problem, I'll walk you through it.

First you will need a computer and internet access. If you don't have that, then go to your local library and get online there.

Most of us already have a personal email address like yourfullname@gmail.com but you'll need to create an entirely new one and one that is in no way associated with your personal one.

This email address will be used to go to free tutorial sites that will teach you how to profit from the internet. Before they will provide that information, you will be required to submit your business email address so they can forward the info to you.

This is why that business address should be completely independent of your personal one. And don't conned into thinking that your computer will be hacked or your identity stolen. My business address czarrichards@gmail.com has been available on my sites for years and I've not had a problem.

Besides, the overwhelming majority of these sites use an auto responder like aweber and get response. Both are very reputable companies and provide a **unsubscribe** link at the bottom of every email you receive. So should you decide you are no longer interested in hearing from a particular website, you can hit the unsubscribe link and you won't be contacted by them again.

But that's rarely needed. If you don't convert into a customer within a certain amount of time, you'll likely be edited out of the email list. Okay, so you've set up a business email address. Great! Now is the time to begin thinking of what type of niche you can make money with.

A niche is the business you want to get into. As mentioned earlier, I'm a writer and book publisher and that is my niche. I don't sell customized sneakers, model airplanes, vacation packages, medical services, weight loss products, dog training tutorials or rare coins.

What I do is write and publish novels and offer my publishing services to professional people looking to establish themselves as an authority by having a book published in their name that outlines their industry and their personal knowledge regarding it... My business address is www.aripublishing.com

So while considering possible niches to get into there are two things *YOU ABSOLUTELY NEED TO KNOW* before you get started.

One: You will hear countless suggestions that you should follow your passion. This isn't quite the great idea it's cracked up to be. What if your passion is Antarctic folk dancing? Making mud pies or lion taming?

You may love doing a certain thing but unless it provides you with a reasonable income it is a hobby not a job. Hobbies you can do in your spare time, however if your serious about making money online you won't have any time for them for the first year or so. Once you get going, and have a firm understanding of how to generate income online, you'll likely have plenty of money and ample time to do what you like.

But not now.

Another thing you need to know is that the majority of online businesses fail. And it's primarily because those people got into online business because they believed it would make them rich with little effort and expense.

Unfortunately, there are hundreds of online websites promising just that! Quick money with little to no effort.

They are all crap so don't be fooled, regardless of how convincing they are.

This is NOT to say there aren't various products and services available that are worth every dime and more. I have bought hundreds of dollars' worth of products and services over the years and each one of them helped me develop and expand my business. These sites have sterling reputations and thousands of members. But they are only valuable to specific online businesses with specific online niches. It is definitely not 'One Size Fits All.'

So that's why it is so important to find yourself a money making niche. The most popular and profitable niches are weight loss, dog training, health, relationships and making money.

But they also have the highest rate of competition. So I would hold off selecting any of those until you have a firm grasp of SEO (Search Engine Optimization) and have learned the art of drilling down to profitable sub niches. In addition, you will need to learn the art of keyword selection. I'll explain. When a person wants to know something or buy something the first thing they usually do is go to Google and type in the thing they want to know about. That is known as a keyword.

Say for example I have an unruly dog, so I type "Dog training" in the search box and I am instantly transported to Google's first page on that topic.

There I will find the most popular and most visited websites with the best rankings that have **Dog Training**, as a keyword in their site. For example, a site titled, *Dog training for older dogs,* or *Dog training in ten minutes*, or *Learn dog training at home* would likely be featured on that first page.

Those seeking specific information on dog training would likely click on those sites and if they have a decent sales page, buy the product.

And that, my friend is your goal. To find a niche and keyword(s) that satisfies the needs of consumers wanting to buy what you have to offer, but has little to no competition. This won't be easy and I don't suggest you get into the dog training field because the competition is monstrous. What I do suggest is that you start looking around. And think outside the box.

There is a famous story where a new marketer noticed that many of the new rappers were sporting jeweled 'grills' tooth caps. So he found a supplier and became an affiliate, created a website, promoted it on all the rap music sites and made over ***One Million Dollars*** in sales in less than a year.

Another bought a popular but abandoned website at auction, then turned it into a stop smoking site that promoted electronic cigarettes. So far he's made over $600,000. I will point out that he is an experienced affiliate marketer and it wasn't his first website by any means. He had his share of failed sites as he learned the business but once he did he's made money ever since.

The learning curve is simply this. In order to be successful online it's always good to learn from the pros and once you get an idea of what you're doing, you have to develop your own system and your own personal style.

Most importantly you need to establish yourself as a reputable business and one that always adds a little extra to ensure customer satisfaction.

So once you decide on a niche, have checked the amount of competition, and have discovered a popular keyword with low competition, then build a site, upload it online and start learning how to drive traffic to your site.

Once again YouTube can help with that.

Don't be scared off by the jargon I'm using. I promise you that NONE of what I'm suggesting you do is difficult to learn or requires a particular skill or educational background.

What it does require is hard work, determination, and a willingness to follow instructions from proven professionals and most of all, staying within the confines of your chosen niche until it becomes either a success or failure. If a success then start up scaling it, if a failure, it's back to the drawing board.

Until you start earning a real income online, I strongly advise you NOT to create your own marketing strategies until you have a built a solid foundation and have a firm grip on what you're doing, THEN, that's the time to explore the vast opportunities the internet provides because by then you'll know enough not to fall victim to paralysis by analysis. (I'll explain what that is later.)

Another option is to open an online store. This is done by creating a name for the store that would receive a lot of keyword searches with little competition. Then go to a domain name provider like namecheap.com and see if the domain name you've chosen is available. I own a website called www.czarscoolstuff.com I rarely use it anymore and will probably sell it because I created it before I really knew what I was doing.

And that's fine! In order to be successful you have to take chances. The website cost me about twenty dollars total and I made the money back in affiliate sales to cover that expense. No harm no foul and I learned how to create my own website.

Now here's the way to make money with your own website. There is a process called affiliate marketing. Here's how it works. Say you create a website called www.pattyO'furniture.com and you want to sell patio and deck furniture on your site.

Here's what you do. You go to the websites of stores that sell a lot of patio and deck furniture. Take Walmart, Target and Amazon for example. If you go to their website home page and scroll down to the bottom, you will see a link that says Affiliates or Become an Affiliate.

What you do is click that link and join. You will be issued an affiliate link that you (or the company itself) will attach to the end of the product link that you intend to sell at your online store.

So here's what happens. On your website you write a review of whatever product you're selling on your site. Say a five piece black lacquer table and chairs with embossed cushions and optional fire pit called the Black Lacquer 5000. You include a large photo of the set and at three places in the review you include the link. For example:

"There are few thing I enjoy more than sitting in my backyard on a summer evening and enjoying the sounds of nature. But in order to be comfortable and relaxed you need the right type of deck furniture (insert you affiliate link here)

Then you go on blah, blah, blah, then midway through you say, but the best one I've found is the Black Lacquer 5000. (Insert affiliate link here)

Then at the end you wrap it up with something like: SO if you're like me and enjoy those beautiful summer evenings then buy the Black Lacquer Deck set with optional fireplace. (Insert affiliate link here) You'll be glad you did!

Now the thing is the more people who see your site the more are likely to buy. So say the deck set sells at Amazon for $399.00 and you get an 8% commission. That's $31.92 you receive for each and every sale.

And that's not all. WHATEVER THAT PERSON BUYS, HAVING USED YOUR AFFILIATE LINK TO GET TO AMAZON, REGARDLESS OF WHAT THE PRODUCT IS, **YOU GET THE COMMISSION**!

So let's say they click on your affiliate link, but decide against the buying the Black Lacquer 5000 but instead purchase a Viking oven and stove top for $2300.00 **you still get a commission check for that purchase**.

So think about that for a minute. What if you have 10 or fifteen or fifty different deck and patio furniture sets displayed on your site from a number of different companies similar to Walmart and Target and Amazon? You have affiliate links attached to every one of them. You have used a number of SEO tactics to increase traffic to your site. You have created an aweber or get response opt-in page to keep your customers up to date on the latest products.

Remember companies like Walmart, Target and Amazon deliver all over the world, to literally billions of people.

I'm sure you get the picture. And that, my friend, is only *one* of the literally thousands of ways you can make money online.

But beware the siren song of big money because there is one deadly enemy to online businesses and it has killed more opportunities than any other.

And it is called ***Paralysis by Analysis.***

"Just what is that?" you ask.

Paralysis by Analysis is discovering that there are **SO MANY** ways to make money on the internet you become overwhelmed! You want to try this, that and the other thing and before you know it you're spread so thin that you can't put in the time necessary to make them all work and so, none of them work and you've just spend a lot of money, and countless hours working on projects that didn't go anywhere and left you with nothing to show for all your effort.

Happens all the time.

Don't let it happen to you.

When you first start out, look for the ways to make money on the net that cost you nothing. Many first timers start out with Travis Sago's BUM Marketing system.

Travis, a very successful internet marketer was often asked for help by people who were flat broke and really couldn't lay out any money at all. So he decided to create a way to make money on the internet, without shelling out any.

He calls it Bum Marketing because with it, any bum could come in off the street and, using this method, start generating some money.

I tried it and it works but it is VERY work intensive. But it did sell me on the fact that there is money to be made on line. And Travis is a great guy. Many internet marketers suggest that as you get started have a look at Travis' Bum Marketing method first.

The second thing you do is go to YouTube and after you finish your daily positive reinforcement video, you start viewing videos from successful internet marketers and see how they do it and what niches they have chosen to make their fortune.

BUT DON'T BUY ANYTHING.

This how Paralysis by Analysis starts. Some of these people have literally made millions on the internet and they all say you can too just by following their method.

Is it possible, yes. Is it likely, NO!

In order to make real money online you need to learn how it's done. There are no quick ways to internet marketing success unless you have a considerable amount of money to lay out up front to purchase mentoring from a proven internet guru. And the real successful ones charge BIG MONEY!

You see, these professionals have mastered all phases of internet marketing and have likely spent years struggling to build their niche business. Why are they now rich and successful? BECAUSE THEY DIDN"T GIVE UP.

When one method failed, they tried another. They went to forums like the Warrior forum and listened to other marketers. They networked and made friends in their niche and learned how to drill down to find a popular uncompetitive niche, created a website and then monetized it.

And when that site takes off they look for the next one and once found, they do the same thing.

So, if you're looking to make money on the net follow these proven methods

DO: Take the time to learn how internet marketing is done. DON'T: Sign up for any internet network that promises to teach you how to make thousands per day by paying them a certain fee every month. I did that and don't regret it ***but***, I could have learned the same techniques by watching **free** YouTube Videos.

DO: Spend time searching for the niche you want to go into. BUT FIRST MAKE SURE IT IS A NICHE YOU CAN MAKE MONEY WITH. The most successful niche website are the ones with the least competition and the most searches. The goal is to get your website listed on the first page of a Google search. Make that happen and you're on your way.

There are a number of websites and YouTube videos that explain how to drill down and find very profitable niches. So focus on doing that first.

Then once you've found a niche you believe you can make money with, you take the next step.

DO: Get a website domain name, purchase webhosting, get a website from Word Press, and then get your site on line. DON'T: Set up your website on a free webhosting site like Blogger or Wix or webhosts like Yahoo. There is nothing wrong with them. I have a very popular blogger website http://zackaryrichards.blogspot.com on Blogger.com and my business www.aripublishing.com is hosted by Yahoo. But the industry favorite is Word Press. It's free and has a huge number of plug-ins that will drive traffic to your site, get you PR ranking and increase your SEO, which is very important to your websites success.

DON'T: Go on a buying frenzy, thinking that each new product related to your niche will attract thousands of visitors that immediately convert into customers. The people selling them will swear that they will and provide testimonials to prove it (did you know you can BUY testimonials on line?)

This is not to say there aren't very valuable product out there created by very respectable marketers. I've purchased great products from Eric Holmlund and Alex Becker for example. Received incredible training from Vick Strizheus and received many great products from fellow marketers just for being a subscriber.

So with that in mind lets' go to the next step in affiliate marketing. I've already discussed how to sell physical products through affiliate marketing through Walmart, Target and the like. Now I'm going to introduce you to the place where you can get software and sell it on your site.

The website is called Clickbank and it is the most widely known and used affiliate warehouse for software products. If you go to their site, you can become an affiliate for just about any software product imaginable.

For example: They feature software you can sell in all these niches:

Art & Entertainment, Business investing, computers & Internet, Cooking, E-business & Marketing, Education, Green products, Health & Fitness, Home & Garden, Languages, Parenting & family, Self-Help, Software & Services, Spirituality and New age, Sports, Travel and several more!

In addition the usual commission rate is **50%!** So if you're looking for a product to sell, that's a good place to start.

As mentioned earlier there are many, many ways to make money on the internet and I've only shown you the tip of the iceberg. But I created this book to provide you with a full view of what you can do to create a better, more satisfying life and not as a 'How-To' on internet marketing. Now that I know how much more there is to write about on that topic I'll likely write another book that focuses on the most successful online marketing businesses and how your can a piece of that pie.

In closing always remember that however difficult things seem now, or have been in the past, there is absolute no reason why you can't Start Over and Rebuild your Mind, Body and Finances. I did it by following the methods detailed in this book and by putting in the effort to make the best use of my knowledge and talents. The result was a better life and a successful, fulfilling business.

There is no reason why you can't have one as well.

So go and seek your fortune and future my friend. You now have everything you need.

www.ingramcontent.com/pod-product-compliance
Lightning Source LLC
Chambersburg PA
CBHW050355280326
41933CB00010BA/1470